Mosquitoes

Anika Abraham

Cavendish
Square

New York

Published in 2019 by Cavendish Square Publishing, LLC
243 5th Avenue, Suite 136, New York, NY 10016

First Edition

Website: cavendishsq.com

This publication represents the opinions and views of the author based on his or her personal experience, knowledge, and research. The information in this book serves as a general guide only. The author and publisher have used their best efforts in preparing this book and disclaim liability rising directly or indirectly from the use and application of this book.

All websites were available and accurate when this book was sent to press.

Library of Congress Cataloging-in-Publication Data

Names: Abraham, Anika, author.
Title: Mosquitoes / Anika Abraham.
Description: First edition. | New York : Cavendish Square, 2019. | Series: Creepy crawlers | Audience: Grades K-3. | Includes index.
Identifiers: LCCN 2018024026 (print) | LCCN 2018025457 (ebook) | ISBN 9781502642318 (ebook) |
ISBN 9781502642301 (library bound) | ISBN 9781502642288 (paperback) | ISBN 9781502642295 (6 pack)
Subjects: LCSH: Mosquitoes--Juvenile literature.
Classification: LCC QL536 (ebook) | LCC QL536 .A27 2019 (print) | DDC 595.77/2--dc23
LC record available at https://lccn.loc.gov/2018024026

Editorial Director: David McNamara
Editor: Kristen Susienka
Copy Editor: Nathan Heidelberger
Associate Art Director: Alan Sliwinski
Designer: Megan Metté
Production Coordinator: Karol Szymczuk
Photo Research: J8 Media

Printed in the United States of America

Contents

A mosquito looks creepy.

It has a small body and a long mouth.

The mouth looks like a straw.

5

A female mosquito lays eggs on water.

She can lay many eggs or one egg.

7

The egg **hatches** into a **larva**.

A larva lives in water and eats food.

It then **sheds** its skin.

It becomes a **pupa**.

9

A pupa does not eat.

Soon it changes into an adult mosquito.

11

An adult mosquito has wings.

It is a brown color.

Fish and bats like to
eat mosquitoes.

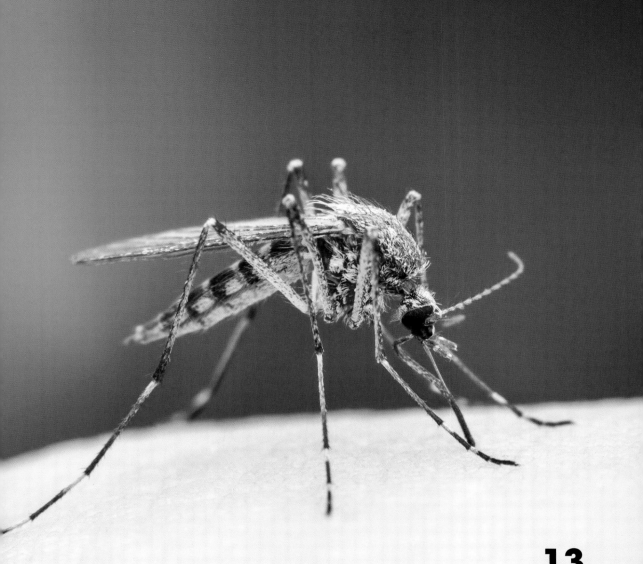

13

A mosquito is very small.

It buzzes around humans and animals.

It likes to drink blood.

15

Only a female mosquito bites.

It bites animals and humans.

It uses its mouth to suck
up blood.

17

Mosquitoes like warm weather.

They live near water.

They fly during the summer.

19

Mosquitoes are not always nice.

They can make people sick.

Do you see any mosquitoes where you live?

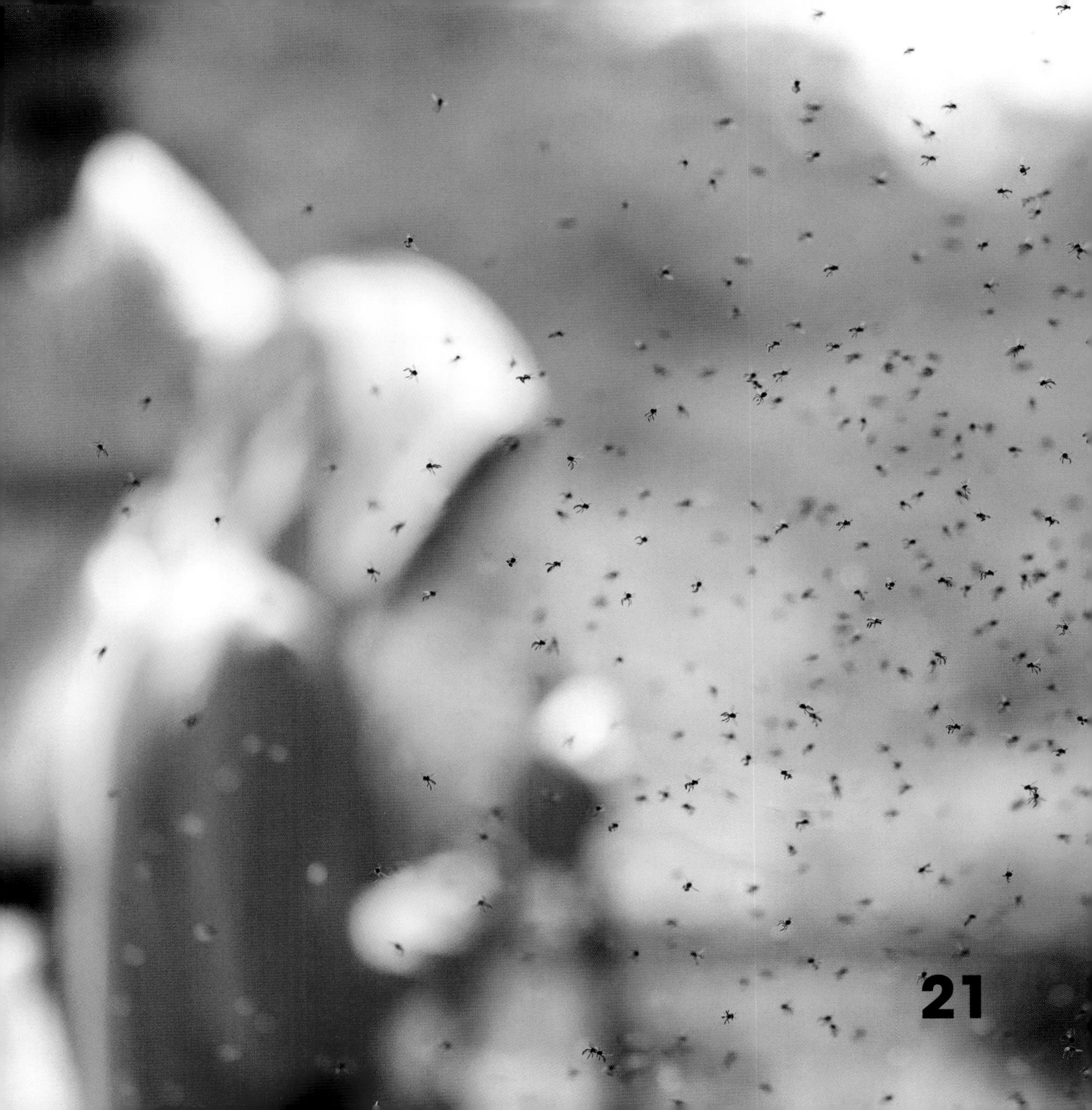

New Words

hatches (HATCH-ez) To leave an egg.

larva (LAR-vuh) A young insect.

pupa (PEW-puh) An insect that is not young or an adult, but in between.

sheds (SHEDZ) When an animal or insect loses an outer layer of skin to make room for a new layer of skin.

Index

23

About the Author

Anika Abraham enjoys the outdoors. She likes learning and writing about animals, insects, and plants. She lives in Chicago, Illinois, with her cat Scrooge and her dog Thunder.

About

Bookworms help independent readers gain reading confidence through high-frequency words, simple sentences, and strong picture/text support. Each book explores a concept that helps children relate what they read to the world they live in.

24